The Best Sex I Never Had:

Secrets & Solace of a Psychotherapist

The Best Sex I Never Had:

Secrets & Solace of a Psychotherapist

Poems by
Susan Black Allen

LEGACY
PUBLICATIONS

The Best Sex I Never Had: Secrets and Solace of a Psychotherapist
© 2025 Susan Black Allen

ISBN: 978-1-962882-09-5 (Paperback)
        978-1-962882-10-1 (Digital)

Cover & Interior Illustrations © 2024 Kelli Urabe

Edited by Jane Foley and Kimiko White
Cover Design by Kelli Urabe
Layout Design by Tiffany Quon

Printed by Jesus Marez
and the Legacy Publications LLC.
Team in the United States of America.
First printing edition 2025.

Legacy Publications LLC.
3422 N. Broadway
Los Angeles, CA 90031

jessemarez@yahoo.com

To Emerson Lindsey Allen, if I had done nothing else positive in this life but create you, it would be masterpiece enough.

Emmy, you are a living, breathing anthology of the finest poetry. Chapters both written and yet to be told. I am so incredibly blessed to be your mother. I love you to the rainbow and back, multiplied by infinity.

To my parents Marvin & Ruth Black, I truly hit the jackpot with you both. You have always supported me, even though you didn't always agree with me or understand me.

Your foundation of love and generosity underlies everything. All of who I am and who I have yet to become. I love, respect and deeply appreciate you more than you will ever know.

Poets are not so scrupulous as you are. They know how useful passion is for publication. Nowadays a broken heart will run to many editions.

Oscar Wilde, *The Picture of Dorian Gray*

May you live a life worthy of poetry. If you are your own best protagonist, others will want to hear your song – and perhaps even sing along.

Susan Black Allen

Table of Contents

The Best Sex I Never Had:

Secrets & Solace of a Psychotherapist

Passion, Relationships, Heartbreak & Love

The Best Sex I Never Had

Overlooking Lago Maggiore's twinkling lights,
our knees brush under the table.
A few drinks in, you confess
that you killed your father.
That his heart stopped because you moved to Brazil
with a woman who would become the mother of
two of your three children.
Your voice still shakes nearly thirty years later.
I take your hand and hold it, repeatedly stroking your palm.

Your sister, my friend,
and her insufferable forever fiancé,
do not notice.

When I share your words later,
they express their surprise.
How'd you ever get him to open up?
"It's a gift, I guess," and shrug.

As we say "Buona Notta"
on the the hotel stairs,
and kiss cheek to cheek to cheek,
a burning zaps down my spine.

And wouldn't you know it,
your room is just down the hall from mine.

I jump into an icy shower,
trying desperately to shut it down.
To put the cap back on the bottle,
the lock back on the gate.

Briskly toweling off and
slipping on a nightie that says,
"someone else's wife,"
I notice a note slipped under the door.

Now in a full on pant,
I remember a time before.
Only one other time,
but enough to know better.

So on the back of your note I write,
"My 18th anniversary means too much to me.
I hope you understand,"
and tiptoe to his door.

There is no sleep to be had that night.
An animal in heat trapped
in twisted, tormented sheets.

Over coffee and croissants,
we pretend it never happened.
Although I flirt outrageously,
telling a story about how I dumped
my first boyfriend at thirteen
and proceeded to date his cousin.

Now you are in your tight swim trunks.
Splayed on the rocks,
like an alpha lion awaiting its next meal.

I step down into the glorious, glacial waters
and slip, scraping my curvy thighs.

I am mortified.
Others notice and comment.
You barely look up.

As I breaststroke large,
looping circles around the pool,
repeatedly drawn closer,
then teasingly further, from you.

Despite the frigid water,
I am on fire.

We return to the hotel to pack,
without you.
You will be meeting friends,
(maybe a woman?)
extending your stay.

As I pack my panties and
spicy orange blossom perfume,

I pen a scented note:
"Thank you for the best sex I never had."

I push it under the door,
part of me relieved.

Part of me, hungry for more.

It's Empty

There's a wine bottle.
Oh look! There's another.
They give a discount on a case?
Guess we can make room.
'Spose that's what your fancy cellar is for.
(As I carry empties out the door.)

There's a wine glass
in the middle
of this marriage.

You have
drained
both.

Dry.

The irony.

Valentine's Day

Love was eating alone one day and choked on a bone.
No one realized it was dead for days,
until the stench became unbearable.

Love was at the park on a Tuesday.
Holding hands one minute.
Sprawled out on the sidewalk the next.
CPR compressions, mouth-to-mouth
couldn't revive it.

Love got up and walked the dog,
got kids ready for the bus, did dishes, the laundry.
While you were fucking
a much younger colleague on a business trip.

Tears, yelling, counseling, lawyers, realtors.
Love taken off life support.
Buried deep in court documents,
sky-high legal fees, child custody arrangements.

Love walked down the aisle today.
Fragrant flowers. Frilly white dress.
Friends and family fawning.
Less than 50% chance of survival.

Let's root for the best.

More Sweet

He asks for the divorce three days after Valentine's Day.
The box of chocolates is still half full.
Not sure if the rest got eaten or tossed.
I do know the "Divorce Diet" is real.

Five years have passed and my love of chocolate
is stronger than ever.
I just put a huge, heart-shaped box in my cart.

Although it has bittersweet moments,
my life is pretty delicious.
This year there will be no dieting
or anything being thrown out.
I have a full box and plan to share.

Dating

Standing on the edge
of the digital shore.
Taut, ready.

Hesitantly, I fling
parts of myself
into the water.

Plenty of nipping guppies,
good time clownfish,
the occasional circling shark.

I'm an excellent swimmer,
not afraid to bite back.

Please
may there be
an angelfish
for me.

Men On Dating Apps

I want a man who catches me a big fish
which he holds proudly next to a fancy boat.

I want a ripped guy on 'roids who flexes for me
and all of Planet Fitness.

I want a dude who raises a beer, a glass of wine,
a round of margaritas. Highlighting
his shot glass collection on his slide show.

I pray for The One who poses seductively
with a come hither stare in his pot-themed jammies,
holding his bong.

I desire a gentleman whose first DM asks me
about my sexual preferences,
specifically, if I'm into anal and BDSM.

I crave a dude whose dick pics look curated,
professional, not digitally enhanced.

I know he's out there.

I just haven't gotten lucky.

Yet.

No Ticket Given

Your hybrid car becomes a motel
by the hour, more like by the minute,
as cars drive by, lights illuminating
steamy windshield.

A man casually gets his mail
while seats are thrown back,
clothes hurriedly hitched up,
dragged down.

Hands and mouths doing what
hands and mouths came to do
when want and need collide.

Breaths high, then higher.
Sounds deep, then deeper.

I imagine a bemused
baby-faced officer fresh out
of the academy
knocking against the window,
flashlight aglow on
moist middle-aged flesh,
asking to join the fun.

"Yes! Yes! YESSSSS!"

The bucket seat
lives up
to its name.
(Hint: we should have used a towel.)

Salsa Picante

I'm the salsa picante
to your giant chimichanga.

The demitasse of espresso
to your double-wide cannoli.

The ripest of juicy mangos
to your friendly green banana.

The warm, saucy Crème anglaise
drip, drip, dripping off your spoon.

Good God,
Let's eat already!

The Math of Middle-Aged Love

Three kids: 19, 16 and 14.
Daughter (mine).
Sons (his).
Two high-maintenance cats (mine).
Dog that chases anything that moves (his).

Two homes overflowing with Tupperware,
underwear and where-did-this-come-from-ware.

Two exes.
His, seen at weekly soccer games next to her boyfriend.
The one she cheated with.
Mine, in secondhand updates
about dad's pot use and dating TMI.

Middle-aged love is two people
figuring out how to start over
one Tupperware container,
one soccer match,
at a time.

An Apology

I am sorry.
I take full ownership,
full responsibility for
my part
in breaking your heart.

When I'm in, I'm 169% in.
I know I can be a lot.

In hindsight, I shouldn't have moved in.
You said you wanted it,
you said you wanted me,
but there were "tells,"
subtle signs
if we are both unflinching honest,
you weren't ready.

Like the slightly shocked,
"Wow, this is really happening,
I'm not so sure about this happening…"
tone of your voice
when you told people
I was moving in.

In my want, in my need
to be wanted, to be needed,
I chose not to see.
I chose to NOT see.
And that's on me.

I chose to move forward apace,
my all-in, leap-of-faith-pace.

I tried to take my place
in a kitchen that you kept
repeatedly pushing me out of,
a table I kept trying to
squeeze conversation into
around the piles of bills
and junk mail
that after about 9 months,

I finally moved to
a nearby chair.

I embraced your sons as my own
Buying them sneakers,
paletas, a snow tubing pass
that never got used.
Picked them up from practice,
cheered enthusiastically at all their games
in a ball cap, gloves, and sunscreen.

I even gave myself a ring,
three mismatched sapphires,
one for each of our kids
which you put on my finger
over Greek Chicken
before a virtual telehealth
appointment in my car.

I gave you one, too,
a black rubber circle
to keep your wonderful,
working-man hands, size 12 fingers safe.
The guys razzing you about
it at JP's over beer.

And I meant it.
Please know that I meant it.
Ms. 169% that I am.

But when the steak isn't
hot enough off the grill,
or I can't read your mind
about wanting breakfast,
or you announce,
yet again that you do
"everything around here,"
not noticing the clean sheets
beneath you,
I crumble.
I come undone.
And it's done.
But this is not about that.

It truly isn't.

It's about me
apologizing to you.
I knew you weren't ready for me
like I wanted you to be.
Like I needed you to be.

I just wanted it so bad.
So, so bad.

But that's on me.
Not you.

I hope next time you are more ready.
And we both know there will be a next time.
Without that ring,
the girls at JP's are already circling.

As for me,
I'm going to love words
exclusively for a while.

That way no one gets hurt.

The Man Who Could Fix Anything

I once knew a man who could fix anything.
For a time, I gave him my heart.

True, he was mechanically gifted.
Leaky faucet, check.
Broken bike, surfboard, catalytic converter.
Check, check, check.

Yet when I gently suggested
he fix himself,
all tools offered
were angrily tossed.

Now my memories of us
are stored on a shelf.
One I ineptly installed myself.

Things Said During the Move

If I ever move in with another man or buy another dress,
I hope you guys will stage an intervention.

My female friends are all so wonderful,
I kind of wish I was a lesbian.

I'm waiting to hear back from my doctor about herpes.
Everything else came back negative.

I've murdered enough innocent plants today.
This one here, you're getting a reprieve.

I never wanted all these pots.
A neighbor left them on the curb.
He told me to take them, so I did.
I'm putting a sign on them saying:
"I'M FREE!"

The ball-chucker and frisbee are for the dog
I'm really (sniff) really (sniff)
(sob) (sob)
Where are the tissues?

Do you want these plastic sushi ornaments?
They were going to be stocking stuffers for the boys.

I like how you curse, Marianne.
It's so authentic.

Fucking Nissan Sentra, trying to cut us off!
Can't you see we're in a fucking U-HAUL?!

X-Rated

A heart beats
between my legs

but no one else
can hear it.

And if I want,

I get lucky
every
      every
            every
      every

Tiiiiiiime…

Residue

There is residue of you on my walk
from the dealership to
The Original Pancake House.
Mouth watering in anticipation
of delicious, overpriced apple crepes.
Abruptly I recall how stone fruit
closes up your throat.

I pass the all-you-can-eat
Korean barbecue joint,
where we took the kids.
Someone's birthday,
I don't remember who.

And there's the karaoke place
with private rental rooms.
I serenaded you badly, with gusto,
in front of all your friends.
"Wise men say, only fools rush in..."
You smiled and nodded in my direction.

As I beamed, a picture was taken.
My spare tire spilling out
over the top of my jeans,
stealing the show.

Somi-Somi is across the street where
I met your boys for the first time
over soft serve in an odd
fish-shaped cone.
Your oldest was chatty.
The youngest in a cast
(skateboard accident).
I loved them instantly,
their sweet earnestness.
I loved how clearly
you loved them.

Like the cone, I overflowed.
Was hooked.
How bittersweet it is, I think,

as I eat my apple-studded,
anaphylaxis-free breakfast.

Placing finger, after finger
of creamy crepe residue
into my mouth.

Wiping the plate clean.

Men & Coffee

I like men and coffee
hot.
No, that's a lie.

Beauty is manifold.
Not simply
base aesthetics.

Pretty boys
often offer ice.
Freezer-burn hearts.

Make mine
complex heat.
Going down smooth.

No bitter bite.
No nasty
after taste.

Don't Fall in Love with Me

Don't fall in love with me
Now's not the time
I will destroy you
Criminal, crime.

Wasn't always this way.
His golden nurse
Patching up brokenness
Praised for the curse.

Then something crucial cleft,
Bird from a cage
Wings flap, flap flapping
Heart full of rage.

Outta the ICU.
Please stay away.
I'm rebuilding my nest
Fine orbs to lay.

Of course, if you're patient
Perhaps you may
Gently offer me gifts
Well-seasoned hay.

But you've been warned.

Love's a long ways
away.

Hetero Guy's Fantasy Dating Profile

I love sex.
Especially blow jobs.
They're one of my specialties.

Threesomes? Sure thing.
My best friend Cheryl is always good to go down.
Err… get down.

She and I met when we were
Dallas Cowboy Cheerleaders.
Believe it or not, our uniforms still fit.

With a little help from Dr. Stein's
"Mommy Makeover" package,
everything's all nice and tight.
(Yup, down there, too.)

That giant fish from your profile?
Cheryl's a gourmet sushi chef
and will turn it into delectable sashimi.

Me, I've always adored housework:
washing dishes, doing laundry,
cleaning toilets in the nude.

When it comes to golf,
Cheryl's better at swinging a club,
but I've always been Daddy's caddy.

And no need to worry about me complaining
about you watching football all weekend.
Having KNOWN many of the players intimately,
Cheryl and I are both passionate about the game.
Oh, did I mention that I'm independently wealthy?
My beloved, late husband left me "We Blow Shit Up."
His national chain of weaponry and firework stores.

His demise. Your gain.

I Want

I want to nibble
on his bushy eyebrows
moving my mouth
down his eyelids,
his eyelashes.
Lush spider webs
against my lips.

I want to remove his hat,
free that dark riot of hair.
Gently scratch his scalp,
looping curl after curl
around my pinkies,
like a prayer.

I want his pupils to dilate
into dark moons.
For him to wax with longing
under the press of my thighs.
For his ear ridges,
ripe on my tongue,
to echo with moans.

I want to suck the salt,
the scent, off his neck.
Leaving slithery trails,
traces of me.
A hungry snail
on a forbidden path.

I want to bury my head
deep into his chest.
Hear his escalating heart,
its elevated cadence,
under my complete, competent,
all-encompassing control.

I want to take him down.
But before I do,
I take his long fingers
show him how

to take care
of me, too.

A
fait
accompli.

Breathless.
Satisfied.
Insatiable.

Más,
por favor.

Young Bull, Old Bull

Young bull, old bull.
I want them both.

In the green pastures of life,
there are lots of cow pies.
Steaming piles of manure,
nose-pinchingly sweet
mounds of used hay.

I used to give them a wide berth.
Turn away with disgust, disdain.

But now that I am no longer fertile,
I seem to seek them out.
Like a toddler inexplicably drawn
to play in the mud.

———

The young bull says to old bull,
"Let's race down the pasture to the Ladies."
The old bull replies,
"Nah, that'll scare them.
Let's walk. Save our energy."

Advice from a seasoned cow to them both:
Stay on your hill.
Smell great. Strut a little.
Rest assured,
we will come to you.

I Have Condoms

I have condoms in my purse.
Magnums purchased by a Mormon
who proudly referred to his penis as Thor.
To his credit, it was quite the hammer.

I dumped him as soon as he
showed me a picture of himself
in authentic KKK regalia on Halloween.

"It was a joke ten years ago," he asserted.
"I'm Mexican," he pleaded.
"You gotta give me some grace…"

Not sure where the condoms are headed next,
but my pussy is not nearly as confused as his cock.

I'm only sad I left my lube behind.
That shit is expensive.

Ice Cream

You melt me like ice cream,
sticky and sweet.

Together we're quite
the lip-smacking treat.

Another serving, please.

Extra sauce, extra nuts.

Self-restraint doesn't apply
to lovers like us.

I Watch You

I watch you.
Breath, rising, falling.
Blessed, blissed out post-coital recovery.

I inhale you.
Your sweet mossy, musky scent.
Like lying in grass with fireflies on a warm summer's eve.

I touch you.
Stroking the soft, downy fur of your arm.
Like my new puppy but without sharp, playful teeth.

I kiss you.
Gentle, oh so gentle, not to wake you.
Your skin tastes like honey pulled fresh from the hive.

Together, we are glorious.
Bodies entangled like a puzzle.
A riddle not needing to be solved.

Nature & Animals

Cowles Mountain

Wild rosemary wafting,
spaghetti fragranced air.
California quail
pit-pit-pitting
a-scramble
under manzanita
quite a charming alarm.

The first time I was left behind.
Pandemic, post-divorce body
panting, lightheaded
on the side of the trail
in search of nonexistent shade.

A stranger stopped,
asked me if I was okay.
I said, I was. I wasn't.

With a dizzy, trippy force of will
I made it to the top
where my then lover
was drinking water,
taking in the view.

The second time it was with you.
We started early and took our time.
Had a dog to help with gravity
going up the inclines.
Reaching the top together
felt triumphant.

But you wanted more.
"Let's do Pyles," you say.
We'd already done
North and South Fortuna.
Pyles would get us to four.
Add Kwaay Paay,
we'd get the coveted certificate.
You were insistent.

"My cranky toe is acting up.
My stomach is starting to growl.
Pyles is too much today.
Can't we please head down?"

You are disappointed.
I sense it throughout the descent.
You are used to getting your way.
You didn't. Turning the day sour.

Now on my third time,
I'm hiking on my own.
But I'm far from alone.

There are young women
in black hijabs resting,
gossiping on the rocks.
There's a shirtless, buff Sailor
in Navy shorts and tattoos
double-timing it past me,
glistening in the sun.

Words float by in Russian, Italian.
Spanish, lots of Spanish.
Occasional Duolingo catching my ears.

From one of my fellow travelers
I overhear, "You're crossing into territory
you don't want to fucking cross,"
as our paths briefly intersect.

As I summit and happily catch my breath,
a girl proudly announces:
"Today's my mother's birthday!
We climbed the mountain to celebrate!"

I offer my congratulations
while thinking:
Today is my birthday too.

It's actually several months away.
Yet today is as good as any other day,
when you're being reborn.

I've Pollinated Your Garden

I've pollinated your garden.
Flitted from flower to flower.
Visited the orange tree
repeatedly,
the one that refuses to die.

I am Worker. I am Queen.

I've made you honey.
Such sweet, sweet juicy honey.

God knows I've tried,
I really tried.
But a different hive is calling,
a new place to call home.
A place less domesticated,
more wild.

Please enjoy what I've sown.

To All the Pets I've Loved Before

To all the pets I've loved before
Forever waiting at the door
I dedicate these words
Perhaps it seems absurd
To all the pets I've loved before.

To all the dogs I've loved before
I rubbed your bellies on the floor.
I've picked up lots poop
We've walked loop after loop,
To all the dogs I've loved before.

To all the cats I've loved in kind
2 a.m. meowing, nearly lose my mind
I've snuggled with you so,
You always seemed to know,
To all the cats I've loved so kind.

To all the ones who've crossed on over,
I hope you're playing in a field of clover.
Princess, Lucy, Rambo, Greta 2,
Please know I remember you.

I dedicate these words,
perhaps it's for the birds,
but our love was true.

To all the dogs that were not mine,
but I loved you in good time.
Satchel with the little legs
and Nova with big sweet eyes.
Your person shared my heart,
but then we came apart
and you had to stay behind.

To all the creatures big and small
Please know that I loved you all.
I dedicate these tears,
feel me scratch behind your ears
and throw you a tennis ball
in my mind.

There's a Tree

There's a tree
with its core cooked.
Crispy center like charcoal.

One stray strike
on a soupy summer day
burned its heart away.

Tiny green shoots
still appear
each spring.

Its branches
forgot how
to die.

Cairn

Strong. Foundation.

Rock on top
of rock.

Pile keeps
getting
hea
vi
er,
high
er.
Thin
ner, wob
bli
er
air
Bound.

Hear
the s
O
u
N
d.

Wh e
n

It all falls…

There's an Oasis

There's an oasis in the desert.
No figment of imagination,
I've seen it twice.

Virginity is overrated.

The second, as sublime,
if not more so, than the first.

This crevice,
where the earth climaxes,
verdant Eden green dancing,
taunting fifty shades of greige,
thirsty desolate dirt.

You show me your oasis,
I'll show you mine.

Nothing like going straight
to the source.

If You're Looking for the Sun

If you're looking for the sun
to rise in the West,
you're not going to find it.

Sure, the skies will slowly brighten
the colors shifting from
dark, sleepy blue-black
to shades of
milky morning light.

Slowly lifting to reveal
the mountains awakening
from their somnolence,
rubbing their eyes,
peaking themselves
awake.

Looking for the wonder
that is you.

Thrilled you have found
each other.

With all the hills you've climbed,
the sun, with its eye-pinching
flash and brash,
doesn't deserve
all the love.

Dayenu

It would be enough
if my soft forest green fleece
from L.L. Bean
over twenty years old
zipper replaced
due to puppy teeth
still fit
keeping me warm on
this glorious cusp of
All Hallow's Eve.

It would be enough
if the sun-dappled mountains
curved like a woman's
supine body
greeted me
and my milky cup of coffee
offering a backdrop
for winged birds
and my imagination.

It would be enough
if the multitudes of
pines cones
bumpy and dark
holding tight to conifers
quite different from those
of my youth
didn't remind me
of how I painted them
with peanut butter and seeds,
a gift for hungry creatures
in the snow.

It would be enough,
it would all be enough.

But there's so,
so much more,
to be grateful for.

Over
and over
and over
again.

Amen.

The Bees are Swarming

The bees are swarming,
looking for a new home.
I have found mine,
returning to the old.

Sometimes to grow,
you need to spread out,
buzz a lot,
frighten a few people.

Just because
you know how to sting,
doesn't mean
it's time to die.

Gather some friends,
make a lot of noise,
dance under the trees.

Eventually the honey will flow.

Catch a Giant Wave

Catch a giant wave,
ride it ashore.
Return with board
to break.
Float and pray
for more.

Occasionally it will
take you down.
Spin you round.
Scrape the ground.

Bubbles and panic,
fish and froth.

Sometimes,
skill isn't enough.

Life will kill you.
Let's not deny it.

Catch the
wave anyway.

It was made
for you.

With God's love,
ride it!

I Saw a Roadrunner

I saw a roadrunner.
The top of its spiky crown
scurrying among the prickly pear.
The 'Meep meep' of childhood
calling to me.
Pushed anvils,
dynamite,
crushed coyote.
Reborn again and again.

I have heard coyotes here.
Packs of them
signaling their distaste
or horniness,
which could very well
be one and the same.

Once I came upon
a lone, oversized
wolf-like one at dusk.
Holding its ground,
tail flick-flick-flicking.
Daring me with its
glowing yellow eyes
to stay on the path
or worse yet,
turn my back.

Unexpected guttural growls
rise up
as I rush him,
boots stomping,
arms flailing.

Unperturbed,
he slinks off into
the overgrown grass
silk rippling.

Neither of us
the roadrunner
this time.

Beaver Mothers

Beaver mothers care for their male pups,
waiting on them hand and foot,
or at least forepaw to tail,
for two years from
the date of their birth.

On their second birthday,
they wipe their fishy claws
and stop.
Stop feeding them.
Stop cleaning up after them.
Just stop.

Mama is officially done.
Junior now is entirely on his own.
He has to fend for himself.

"We find many dead juvenile males every year,"
the park ranger explains.
"A lot of them just don't figure it out."

Maybe human mothers need to do the same.
Say when they turn 16.

We'd all likely be better off for it.

But I'm the mother of a daughter.
So my vote probably doesn't count.

I Chose Not to Kill

I chose not to kill the spider.
Although I've crushed
many in my day.
He looked small, vulnerable.

I opted to give him
the power
this time.

It's Raining in San Diego

It's raining in San Diego.
No one knows what to do.
The sky is falling, the sky is falling!
A modicum of liquid and we curl up
into our sweet SoCal shells.
All sunshine and sugar skulls,
look out, we might melt.

But can you blame us?
BMWers and Chargers careening
into muddy ditches, military parade.
Racing testosterone,
limited frontal lobe development,
full hydroplane salute.

Even the Zoo is in uproar,
watery wartime dispute.
Gorillas pounding their chests
demanding umbrellas.
The elephants trumpeting
the benefits of galoshes.
Escapee I.B. flamingos
booking first-class tickets to Bora Bora.

Only the inhabitants of SeaWorld are overjoyed.
Delighted dolphins dancing raindrops.
Stinky sea lions shower singing.
Rays rejoicing in the gray,
fewer hands in the touch pool today.

Yes, it's raining in San Diego.
Time for frost-hardened transplants
to amusedly shake our heads.
As wimpy natives and bored,
ratings-starved meteorologists
pour it on thick.

Cut Back the Roses

We gather round as
the Head Gardener announces,
"This is NOT how you prune roses,
people."
He takes delicate shears and
proceeds to perform
minor surgery
on the bush before us.

"This! This is how you do it!"
He drops the clippers
and in one swift yank brings
a chainsaw roaring to life.

He takes that plant
nearly to the ground.

My life, I muse.
Canes, broken buds
toppling.

Bless and sharpen
the blade.

Taking Grace

Stolen oleander picked
on a public path.
Birds chirping their consent.
Rabbit wiggling its nervous nose in dissent.

I hear mother and child giggling,
as I tuck fresh buds behind my ear like a new bride.
I am selfish and continue picking —
empty vases waiting to be filled.

"You are encouraging them to grow," my cousin Nina proclaims.
"You're scrumping!" My ex's British best friend announces
in accented approval.
Their voices reach me across land and sea.

Nice to hear, but I don't need anyone's blessing —
to claim my place,
to take a little grace
for myself.

I Want to be in the Clouds

I want to be in the clouds.
Light pouring from my fingers
pooling between my legs,
little pop-pop-pops
of renewable energy
exploding the length of
my knobby spine.

I am so weary.
So, so weary.

Maybe you are too.

Let's climb up
to the clouds
together.

Create a new kind of weather.

Chiaroscuro for me and you.

Lay Me Down

Lay me down
in a field of lavender.
Fill my pockets, my hair,
my mouth,
all of me,
with blossoms
like a sachet.

Let me be
a giant nose
bursting to explode.

God,
if I have to go,
may it be
in such a
sweet smelling
way.

A Little Wild

I recognize the wild in her.
The urge to sniff,
nose intent in the bushes,
gliding along glorious textures of the ground.

Both predator and prey,
eternally embedded in our DNA.

The urge to lick, to chew, to bite.
Rough pink puppy tongue,
sharp teeth seeking solace,
in pressure, in presence.

A face, an elbow, a stick.
Part oral pleasure, part pain,
a timeless mammalian refrain.

Followed by kisses.
Always followed by kisses.

There's another bitch in the house.
She sees me as her Master.
I see her as my blessed doppelgänger.

As I inhale her sweet-sour fur,
I realize,
we're both right.

I Took the Loquats

I should have asked,
but they hung abundantly
over the fence.
Yellow-orange clusters
calling "yes, yes, yes!"

Not for me, but for Jeff.
A dear friend back East
who once warmly reminisced
about eating them
on an Israeli commune
in his twenties.

Now in his seventies,
how many seasons of loquats
does he have left?
How many
do any of us?

A mouthful of memories.
Stolen, sweetness of life
sent FedEx direct.

What Will It Take

What will it take
to convince you to live?
To REALLY live.

Which inspired words
will plant the right seed?

In soil so depleted,
in a world
so deeply depleted,
is that even possible?

I hear coyotes laughing.

The desert teems with life.

Therapy –
Theirs & Mine

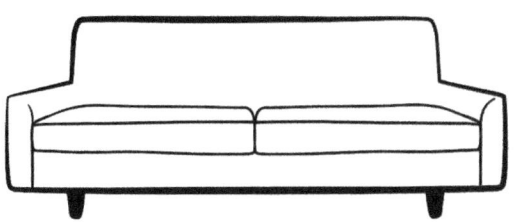

Mary, Christie, Jess, Leslie

1.

Mary, I think
that was your name.
I was a very, very
sad young woman
sobbing in your office,
ashamed to be in your office
and not there for myself,
but for Donna,
my sophomore roommate,
cheery sunshine to
my never-ending sky of dark clouds.

You were the first one to
give it a name.
To give me a diagnosis.
When you said the d-word,
I felt relieved.
A word for all the pain in my head
that wasn't just in my head.

You looked so weary Mary.
Week after week,
all us Wheaties
(that's what we called ourselves)
with our tears, trauma, and youthful drama.
Mary, you helped put a word
to why I wanted to die.
Which may have kept me alive.
Thank you.

2.

Christie, Oh Christie…
I saw your obit online.
You were not young,
but you still left us before your time.
Christie, you looked me in the eye
and told me point blank:

"I don't think I can help
you if you don't go on medication."

In my sleep-deprived, devastated state,
these were not words I wanted to hear.
But my stubbornness had softened enough
from my colicky daughter's tears,
co-mingled with my own,
to actually listen.

I remember the exact moment
when the meds started to kick in.
I was in the kitchen making a bottle.
As the sun came up, the following words rose
with my rising neurotransmitters:

"This is still really, really hard,
But I am going to be ok.
We are going to be ok."
My cheeks wet with tears.

Christie, my now 21-year-old daughter and I
Thank you.

You said the hard thing, the true thing.
And as saying hard, true things
always does, it made all the difference.

3.

Jess, with your curly, crazy hair,
artsy office and earnest eyes,
you listened about my clients
while I was your client.
An experienced therapist
supporting a newbie
with warmth, wisdom, and kindness.

You listened to me as I read
the words I had written
and reacted like they were
worthy of an audience.
You told me I was worthy, too.

Jess, you were so sincere,
I believed you.
You built me up
like excellent therapists do.

We shared stories of our shared
Seasonal Affective Disorder.
You understood when I said:

"I don't think I can live here anymore,"
after a winter with 110 inches of snow.

You blessed my decision to move
which helped me hold firm
against all the naysayers.
All the well-meaning crabs
trying to pull me back
into the proverbial pot.

Thank you, Jess.
Your clients are blessed.
I'm glad to have been one of them.

4.

Leslie, dear, dear Leslie.
I had the great, good fortune
to find you soon after moving
to Our Finest City.
Your gentle questioning and unfailing support
welcomed me to this hospitable climate
where I quickly and joyfully put down roots.
You've watched as I made friends,
found work, built a life.

But Leslie, you and I both know
it hasn't exactly been 'California Dreamin.'
You remember my psychopath bully of a boss
who told me I was "too sensitive"
when I said a domestic violence video of
someone being choked out was disturbing.

Or the sister-like relationship that
collapsed on what was supposed
to be a dream girls' trip to Europe
when she tolerated his abuse,
because it was less scary, easier,
then standing up for me.

Oh yeah, and then there was
the implosion of my nearly 22-year marriage.
A union that had been dissolving for years
from my ex's love of fine wine,
finally burning up in his bong.

God bless you, Leslie!
I don't know how I would have survived
all of it without you.
You have been a godsend.

Actually, since you are about to call me
for our regularly scheduled appointment,
I will go ahead and thank you now.

Emotions

I have more than my share.
From the day I exploded from
my mother's womb
uttering a harsh wail,
I have filled the room.

An energetic,
palpable
Here I Am
BOOM!

No dimmer switch
have I.
No way to hide the
huge emotions
shifting the tide.
More roller
than coaster,
it makes for quite
a ride.

I can be
exhausting
even to myself.
But how do you
put intensity
on a shelf?
In some ways,
it's a form of wealth.

The gold of poets
and mad men
alike.

As long as I am able
to mine it,
not be buried
alive.

I Once Wanted to Die

Layer upon layer of skin
vulnerable, opaque.
Even my eyelashes ached.

An Everything, Everyone-Sponge.

Like a giant Saguaro,
outstretched, thorny arms,
growing swollen, wretched,
in a never-ending storm.

The storm clouds, you see,
self-seeded within me.
A toxic stew of biochemistry.

Now every night,
I take a little white pill.

The rains still come,
but my brain drains better.
The neurotransmitters flow.

I once wanted to die.

Now I dance in puddles.

An Everything, Everyone-Rainbow.

Your Story

You have fifty cents in your bank account
and visit food pantries
while I sip a latte at Starbucks
and glance at my gold watch
wondering when Merry Maids will be done.

But every week for fifty minutes,
we are together.
My office, your stories.
Stripped raw of circumstance, of formalities.

You tell me about your alcoholic parents
and money begged from strangers
when you were ten
that ended up buying booze instead of food.

You tell me about the uncle who molested you.
He violated your cousins, too.
Your parents buying their parents' secrecy.
How you cried when they moved out.

You tell me about sniffing glue.
How if the lights weren't on after school,
it meant your mother had passed out.
At sixty-five, you are still afraid of the dark.

You tell me about no heat, no electricity.
How you saved your money to replace the record
your father smashed in a rage.
Hoping your mother might listen
to their favorite song again.

You tell me about selling drugs
and how you tried not to sell them to other kids.
But if you didn't,
they'd just buy them from someone else.

You tell me about wanting to become
an architect; how you were good at math.
How a friend leaves you in the street after overdosing.
You overhear a doctor say, "This one here, he's gone."

You tell me about the teachers, the probation officers,
the social workers, the detox counselors,
all of whom tried to save you.

When ultimately what saves you
is a chance meeting with a man
with blue eyes in a bar.

It's for Blue Eyes that you get and stay clean
for thirty-five years.
He holds you in the dark and you hold him back.
You cook together. You have cats.
Together you struggle, but your math pays the bills.

Then Blue Eyes gets sick.
A heart big enough to hold the world.
Your world.
But not strong enough to never break.

And now you are in my office.
Thick with grief.
You have relapsed.
You tell me you are not ready to die,
but have just hit a parked car while high.
You are desperate and need my help.

I pray to Blue Eyes that my green eyes are enough.
For this beautiful, broken man,
I hope that I am enough.

Like Roses

I embrace you.
All of you.
Your soft and tender places.
The ones you bury, deep and dark.
Your glassy shards and cactus thorns.
I gather them into my arms like roses.
And we bleed together
until the bleeding stops.

War Zone

He is tall, thin,
intellectual looking,
and wearing a Star of David
and John Lennon glasses.
Eyes red, puffy behind them.

I have lost everything:
My career, my home, my family, my life, he says.
Do you want to die? I ask.
Yes, he says.
Do you have a plan? I ask.
Yes, he says.
How?
Pills. I tried to overdose in Turkey a year ago
and I'm ready to do it again.
My sister and brother are in Russia.
My brother was a soldier,
lost his arm in Ukraine.
My grandmother lives in Ukraine.
The rest of my family is in Israel, in Tel Aviv.
All my loved ones are in war zones
and I can't help them,
he sobs.
I can't help them,
face between his hands.
I yell, hit the walls,
and cry myself to sleep.
I drink myself to sleep.
I can't go back to Russia
I am a political criminal –
spent fourteen days in prison.
I can't go back to Russia.
If I go back, they will kill me.
I would rather kill myself.
I have nothing here.
No job, no friends, no family.
The woman who trafficked me
just got out of jail.
She knows where I live.

I'm so sorry, I say.

You need help, I say.
You are deeply depressed.
Depression can be treated.
In five years things will be different,
things may be better.
I can't help a dead client, I say.
I need to send you to the hospital.
He nods, understands.

I'm sorry it's taking so long,
as I'm on hold waiting
fifteen minutes for the dispatcher
and then another fifteen minutes
for the EMTs to arrive.
I have been with him,
with all of him,
for over two hours.
My stomach is growling,
I need to pee.
But even more
I feel the urge to scream.
To scream at Putin,
at Hamas,
at Netanyahu,
at all the evil,
all the fucking evil
that has crushed this man,
turned his life into a dumpster fire.

While I silently scream and shake
from cortisol rushing through my veins,
I also pray that Mercy Hospital keeps him.
Doesn't turn him away.

Back onto the streets,
victimizing him yet again,
with all
the world's demons
eating him alive.

12 Step Redux
(Inspired by Peter)

God grant me the serenity
to keep my sanity
in a world that's often cruel,
unjust and seemingly blind.

God grant me the grace
to know when to stay,
fight the good fight,
and when
to walk away.
When it's healthier,
for all involved,
not to
turn back.

God grant me the insight
the intuition,
to make the giant two-foot drop
from
my head
to
my heart.

And lastly God,
grant me the cojónes
to *actually* listen.

Therapy Session

"I killed an innocent woman when I was seventeen.
Spent forty-one years in prison, mainly Calipatria,"
says the distinguished, bearded gentleman in bifocals,
who looks a lot like Cornell West,
sitting across from me.

"The seed was planted at age 8 or 9.
I was always pushing the limits.
My parents were working two jobs and had four other kids.
Everything I did was birthed from a lack of attention."

"Once night, my older brother convinced me
to help him break into a liquor store.
I was a skinny kid,
so they lifted me up to the second floor
and I slipped through the bars."

"The guard dogs didn't bother me.
I knew they wouldn't hurt me,
because dogs won't hurt a kid."

"My brother paid me
with a bag of change and a bag of candy.
At school, whenever someone needed a quarter,
I had it to give.
That was my first taste of power."

———

A man with blond kewpie doll hair
and bright blue eyes sits with
a black chihuahua, named Opie, in his lap.
Opie is wearing a bat costume for Halloween,
wings flapping.

"After my mother died, I was living in a riverbed
drinking myself to death.
I woke up one morning,
my face covered in blood,
didn't even remember falling on the rocks."

"Then I lost Opie in an Albertsons parking lot.
I searched and searched and searched.
He was gone.
I went into treatment after losing him."

"Six months later I got an email
from the Humane Society.
Opie was microchipped
and someone had found him.
He was living in foster care."

"I called his foster mom and wanted to lie,
but told her the truth.
That I was an alcoholic in recovery.
I sobbed and sobbed with her on the phone.
She was so kind to me.
She said, 'Do what you need to do
to take care of yourself.
We will take care of him.'"

"Opie's foster mom and her husband
invited all of their friends
to my graduation from rehab.
I cried and cried."

———

A woman who was born a boy
looks out at me from her screen.
I look back at her through mine.

Her long hair is pulled back into a ponytail,
her teeth jagged. A former meth mouth
desperately in need of dentures.
Something I hope she will eventually agree to
as her current diet consists of ramen,
whisky, gallons of whole-fat milk,
and not much else.

"At the hospital, they can never find a vein to draw blood.
All the veins in my arms are shot.
Even the one in my neck is hit or miss.
Years and years of shooting up."

I ask her how much money
she estimates she spent on drugs
before becoming "California sober."

She points to her arms:
"This one here, that's a Porsche.
And that one there, that's a Lambo."

A deep-throated sound rises from her
across our screens.

And together,
we laugh
and laugh.

Santa & Mrs. Claus

He is Santa, a proud motorcycle-riding, Trump-loving,
uncomfortably gay Conservative with twinkling blue eyes,
authentic round belly, and beard.

They are Mrs. Claus, a blonde bombshell,
Express Yourself Madonna drag queen,
convicted sex offender:
videos of marginally underage man-boys.
Nobody,
quote unquote,
was hurt.

Both of them frequent my office this holiday season.

Surprisingly, they are a gift to me.

The depth and breadth of my heart
sometimes gives me pause.

The Lost & Found of Hillcrest

Different day, same souls
wandering the streets
with haunted, terrified eyes,
which I rarely meet as to avoid
possible provocation.

Neither a threat
or potential savior, I.

One of my previously unhoused clients,
tells me with shaking Haldol hands
how he offers to buy a meal
for one of the denizens of the Square.

"I figured they'd want a sandwich or something.
But no, this skinny shirtless guy
wants a Mountain Dew
and a Butterfinger."

"I said to him, 'Are you sure?
I can get you something more…
a sandwich, maybe?'
But he assures me that soda and candy
are enough."

"So that's what I get him.
Because some days,
a Mountain Dew and a Butterfinger,
that's all you really need."

I nod. Amazed at my client's
kindness, compassion, and generosity.
How this once down-and-out man
validates another's humanity.

While thinking
love, caffeine and sugar
are often
what get me through, too.

Green and Growing

"If I'm not green & growing,
then I'm brown and rotting."

A gay, bald bear of a man
announces during our intake.

He's two years sober,
after years and years of meth use.
Previously tried to kill himself
twenty-nine times
after an HIV diagnosis.

"I shouldn't be alive,
but I'm doing great now.
After I decided to live,
I discovered flowers.
Became a florist."

Now, that's one way
to use the manure of
your life, I think.

I want to graft him
onto my other clients.

Maybe all of them
should become
florists.

Three Men Lost

I remember each of your faces.
The bus driver with deeply kind,
deeply sad, blue-blue eyes.

The second with mischievous,
damaged boy energy,
meds temporarily holding back
the itch to get high.

The latest, not likely the last,
a proud Navy veteran,
both victim and alleged perpetrator.
Surprised what he
thought was consensual,
she said was not.
(Both of us were horrified
when I had to share this news,
her version, with you.)

Each of you once
sat in front of me
and now are gone.
Leaving behind people
who loved you.

The husband with his own
thirty years of sobriety
who relapsed, then also became my client,
when he lost you.
(Would I lose him, too?)

The long-term girlfriend
who ran marathons,
you cheering her en route.
She loved you —
missing teeth,
methadone and all.

The young son,
who saw part of the assault
but was told that

mommy and daddy
were "just playing."
Mommy's tears,
Daddy's broken ribs and all.

All three of you walked
through my door
not as addicts,
but as people.
Hurting human beings.

The trauma took you first.
The drugs finished the job.

Please know that
in my heart,
in my work,
each of you
live on.

Forcing the Illness Out

Sometimes my
nervous system
gets sick.

I have to curl up in a ball,
remember how to breathe.

Or lace up
my running shoes
and go-ohhhh…

F***ing hills, humans, hurt!

Panting, sweating, sobbing.
Returns me to myself.

Forces some of the illness out.

If I could just keep it
from getting
back in.

You Can't Make

You can't make a puppy pee.
You can take them outside to their designated spot,
wait patiently while they sniff,
but if they are distracted by a passing car or chirping birds –
pleading that the carpet is new or that you're going to be late,
is not going to make the urine flow.

You can't make a woman,
or a man, leave their abuser.
Lord knows I've tried.
You can remind them of their bruises,
of the cutting, cruel words so much worse than bruises.

You can explain how the flowers, the "I'm sorry's,"
the "I'll never do it again's,"
the "You mean everything to me's,"
are just part of a vicious cycle.

You can even look beyond horrified
when she tells you that he nearly starved her beloved dog
while she was away.
She had to give it away.
And yet she stays.

You can't make animals,
human, or otherwise,
do anything that aren't willing
or ready to do.

However you can secretly plot murder in your mind
while you patiently take your puppy back inside.
To try again later.

Hoping she has a later.
That today is not the day.

How Do You Do It?

"How do you do it?" asks a military wife with several children
and significant adult and childhood trauma.

"How do you deal with people's pain all day long?"

I mention self-care, boundaries, and training.
Standard therapist stuff.

She nods, brushing away tears,
asks if she can give me a hug
at the end of our session.

After our quick embrace, I want to tell her the truth.

My office is like a compost pile for pain.

What breaks down pain?

The same thing that keeps me sane: *Love.*

Sadness, Grief & Tough Stuff

Love Remains

After everything is gone,
love remains.

Love lives in the air that you once exhaled.
It grows in the grass you danced across.
It hides behind downcast eyes
and glows in laughing ones.

Love flows like water from the tap
filling and overflowing,
forming rivulets that quench dry,
thirsty places.
Places where fire has left sleeping seeds
awaiting your touch.

Love flutters like Monarchs
who somehow know
where their delicate, determined
wings must go.

That which once lived in you,
now lives in me.

It breathes life into everyone
who chooses to notice.

Young William

There is a place of rest
tucked in a forest nest.
Few know it exists,
mossy headstones
in the mist.

Amongst the
thorny bramble
and ruby bittersweet,
you might randomly meet
young William, age 14.

Cause of death:
Kicked in the head by a horse.

I imagine his mother
keening on the mound.
Can almost hear the sound.

And wonder:
Who the Hell
picked his epitaph?

Let's Talk About Death

This poem breathes,
has a heartbeat.
Listen closely.
Do you hear it?

When I'm in the
ground stone cold,
She will continue
happily humming
along.

Perhaps
in her pulse,
in her pause,
I will live on.

Or the page
will simply
turn.

Turn me
into a
forgotten
song.

Not if you
continue
to sing
along.

A Mother's Love

If She rejects You,
She may very well
be rejecting herself.

Mirrors we often are
of our mothers.
Our birth rite, our due.

Or crazily, could be the inverse,
you're so different:
She's an elephant, you're an elf.
Too much space between,
a gaping hole to fall through.

If You reject Her,
you may very well
be saving yourself.

Many a daughter has sacrificed
her sanity at the altar of
Maternal vanity.
Or been s-Mothered into
immolation in the name of
familial assimilation.

But perhaps you're simply
being immature, selfish.
Not giving Mom her due.

Depending on the circumstances, either could be true.

If only we could give
elves and elephants magic wands,
then maybe,
just maybe
we'd all get along.

But more likely
chaos
would ensue.

Family Secret

Every family has one,
usually a set,
like mutant china
hidden behind opaque,
ornamental doors,
taken out furtively, regularly
to drink a dark, bitter brew.

Shards cutting with every sip.
Going down, down, down.
Fated for festering;
no hope of digesting.

All Hail the Cup of Shame!

With Blame
plated conveniently
by her side.

Lip service
to protect your hide.

Because of The Losers

Bring me your tired,
your addled, your addicted.
Your burning, hurting masses
hoping to be heard.

Bring me your unhoused,
the rejects,
the folks who have been used,
abused, and repeatedly refused
by blood and system alike.

I am deeply indebted.
Because of the Losers,
Some of Us are Winners.

Listening, loving, respecting.
That's the least I can do.

They take the brunt
for the rest of us.

Could be the other shoe.

The World is Too Hard

The world is too hard
for me.
I need softer edges.

Sand,
not concrete.
Moss,
pine needles.
Not marble,
tile, or laminate.

So when I fall,
and
I
will,

the impact
won't hurt
so much.

Urgent Care

I drove myself
or maybe I was driven.
Sometimes it's hard to
distinguish between the two.
Either way, I am here now.

Doctor angry,
No ambulance called?

My body has taken me
to the ground
not once, but twice.
Ripped shower curtain.
Two lumps, four staples.
Hard to deny the proof.

I have been poked, prodded.
Scanned and monitored.
Ultrasounds, EKGs.

Three days, two nights
they have thrown the
medical textbook at me.

Fancy adjustable bed
(I have to ask to pee),
butt barely covered gown,
gourmet hospital food.

My slightly bruised brain
continues to solve
crossword puzzles,
searching for answers.

From Duolingo, I learn
"levantarse" means to
"get up."

I heard the ultrasound.
It was breathtaking:
Woosh, a-woosha, woosh.

Even while holding my breath,
my heart continues to beat.

I care urgently.
I am urgently cared for.
But something is clearly
taking me down.

Am I betraying myself somehow?
I want a test for that.

Pushing the call button now.

Somebody's Child

Our Lady of CVS holds court daily on her corner.
Caked in dirt and world-weariness.
A dark, woolen blanket around her waist,
even in 90-degree weather.
Her matted, mangy ponytail defies gravity,
offering an "F you!" to the world.

I imagine Our Lady in her Mother's arms
swaddled in a different blanket.
Probably something soft and pink.
Her tiny, tender lips
Searching hungrily for a nipple.
Her unfocused newborn eyes
searching steadily for recognition.

I'm ashamed to admit
I cross the street to avoid her.

I, a psychotherapist,
a Unitarian Universalist,
a bleeding heart liberal.

Our Lady frightens me,
because she could be me.

And that's too heavy
a dark blanket
to bear.

The Game of Life

At birth, dice are rolled for us.
Gifts are given, withheld.
Your move how they're played.

Whether tended like tender plants,
or left to die on the vine.

Agency is everything.
But how much do we actually have?

Work hard, perform.
Pay bills.
Don't drink and drive.

Shitty health card drawn.
Ex takes it all.
Nonverbal autistic child.

No wonder everyone
wants to retreat
down a rabbit hole.

It's tempting to try to escape.

When there's nowhere to hide.

Green-Eyed Monster

She reads her poem
and it is
punch you
in the gut
good.

"Good,"
such a weak, overused word.
Can't you come up with
something better,
anything
more original
than that?

Get out your thesaurus.
You fraud,
you hack.

Never mind,
it's not going to be enough
to save you
from your lack of rhythm,
your oddly structured lines.
Your inconsistent rhymes.

You don't know
what the fuck you're doing.
That fact is readily apparent.

And you're up at 4:30 a.m. losing
precious sleep over this?
Why even bother?

Even if you were any good,
which is highly debatable,
Nobody
buys
poetry books
anyway.

Unless you're
Mary Fucking Oliver
or Maya Angelou —
and they're dead.

So go back to bed.

"No," I said.
"I am worthy," I said.

"Now get the fuck outta my head!"

Left Behind

Sometimes people die
even though
they are still
very much alive.

Denise's mother.
Beth's daughter.
The father of my child.

All alive
and hopefully well.
Off doing whatever
they're doing.

With us left behind.

Sometimes

Sometimes when I am finally
able to rest, to reset,
overthinking gives way
to liquid emotion,
lifelike in its fluidity.

For what else are tears,
but life force clear and wise?

Like blood to the heart,
tears are to the soul.

I make donations regularly
for the unwilling, the unable.

That said,
no martyr,
am I.

No matter
how much
I cry,
I will never,
ever,
let myself

run dry.

Growth, Healing & Spirit

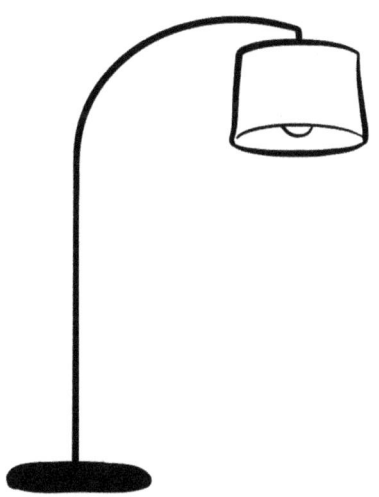

Fall Back

An extra hour seems like a gift.
More time for mom's oatmeal bread to rise.
My version, delicious.
But never quite as good as hers.
Something she does with the dough.
Or maybe it's actually equally good.
But hers is made for me.
Which elevates everything in ways
which simple yeast and flour
by themselves can never do.

An extra hour offers more time for
cuddling a child with a book.
Sweet-scented head tucked up under your arm.
A sacred space, a communion of words, wonder and warmth.
A story within a story within a story
of shared person and place.
As ancient as our ancestors sitting around a fire,
sharing the lyrics, the lore of time eternal.

Another hour for writing a card
curling cursive, sticky stamp, icky lick envelope
for a far away mailbox needing a little extra love.
The surprised recipient finding it nestled
amongst the junk mail and bills
like an unexpected offering from the Postal Gods.
A bridge built with simple paper, ink and goodwill.
Words that may live on long beyond
both the writer and the recipient.
Unlike the buzz of modern electronic communication.

I turn back the clocks as I contemplate
this precious sixty extra minutes.
The car, the microwave, my lovely old gold watch.
If only we could gain, not lose,
an hour of sun with this additional time.
Now that would truly be sublime.

Then I realize, you can always be
your own version of the sun.

Good morning Pancreas

Good morning pancreas,
keeps those juices going.

Hello left ventricle,
how's everything flowing?

Thank you knees,
yesterday's hike was sublime.
Couldn't have done it without you.

Rise and shine shoulders,
I know you're tight.
Shrug that shit off.
Let it go-ohhhhh.

Greetings sweet lips,
I know you miss being kissed.
Speaking the truth can
be lonely sometimes.

But ultimately,
it's much better
for the soul.

Late Day Lotus Rising

Sometimes you have to bounce
Although part of you says,
"Stay. Don't do it.
Keep pretending this is home."

Sometimes you have to toss yourself,
sight unseen, destination unknown,
into the
      abyss.

Every nerve of your body tight, tense
wanting to cling to what's known.
Soft moss beneath you
calling you to rest.

But staying would be a lie, dying bit by bit.
A neglected houseplant. Yellow, listless.
Waiting for rains that will never come.

There's a padparadscha horizon.
Late-day lotus rising.

So you pull up your roots,
(the ones you'd so hopefully planted),
kick the dirt off your skirt,
and offer your arms to the sky.

And *fly*...

The Body is a Sacred Place

I look at my chest
peppered with electrodes.
Wires snake down to my belly.
Feeding a box that measures
pulsating chambers
artery song,
roaring, riotous rivers,
gooey, sweet platelets
type A positive, et al.

I look beautiful.
Like a feminine cyborg.
Frightenedly alive,
fascinating even.
Eyes a bit red, swollen.
Raw, rough-hewn
like a secret temple
where Natives
make sacrifices
of feathers, fruits
and nuts.

There is a needle
embedded in my arm
for easy access.
An addict's wet dream.
It is sterile and awaits
potential disaster.
I am sterile, but having
produced a daughter,
pray disaster
passes me by.

I make ablutions as best I can
with a washcloth and wipes.
Cleansing the trauma and sweat,
from the sacred scent of my skin.
Working around apparatus
with gentle, persistent strokes.

Health isn't always allocated
as expected.
The marathon vegetarian
dead at twenty-four.
The chain-smoking, hard-drinking partier
continuing to play stadiums at eighty.

I have taken you for granted.

It's hard to live every day
in awe of oneself.
But perhaps,
if we worship God,
we can worship God's creation.

Or at least try to more often
than when a hospital visit
calls us out.

We Are All Gamblers

Even the ones who play it safe.
Especially the ones who play it safe.
Those who never
take a chance on love.
Who handle their hearts
with kidskin gloves.

Those whose whole life perimeter
consists of mere miles.
Who don't know beyond which
the ragged crow flies.
Then there are those
who never question anything
they've been taught about life.
Just parrot back words
like holding a knife.

Give me your radicals, your restless, your wanderers.
Those whose wounded hearts have learned
love is a salve that heals much more than it hurts.
Show me the risk-takers who raise their hands
even when those hands are shaking
and speak up when voices are quaking.

We all roll the dice in this life.
Some die are blank.
Some die blank.

Give me double or nothing.

Chimes

As the chimes ring out
another day,
I pause.
Ears delighting
in wind song.

A Cessna
or perhaps a Piper
alights into the brightest
bright to call forth
the cool caress that
we call night.

The bells they ring
no eyes to see,
to know
the rightness
the wrongness
of time or clime.
Ignorant even of
the plane,
its climb.

Some mysterious breath
is all it takes.
To sing, to dance
to shimmy and shake.

Yes!
Some mysterious breath.
That's what we share.

They pause in their song,
and at least
for the moment,

I breathe on.

A Prayer for the Hurting

I've knelt and wept
in the great cathedrals:
Duomo di Milano, Notre Dame,
St. Florin, San Luis Rey.

I've lit flickering candles,
absorbed Gregorian chant.

I've offered up my raw soul
and bruised heart
to the gods and goddesses
pleading that my pain,
the throbbing ache of each of us
is not felt in vain.

As I inhale the pungent scent of lilies
and exhale a heavy breath,
a breath that connects each of us.
Blessed be thy name.

Flip the Coin

Flip the coin of life:
Love heads, tails heartbreak.
Hope heads, tails despair.
Stability heads, tails chaos.

Like a black cat
who gets a bad rap,
I keep on chasing
tail, tail, tail.
A mouse caught,
tossed, in pain

White knuckling the coin,
my luck to change.

Probability in part
being defined
by stubbornness.
Vegas odds,
I own this game.

Cue the dancing
and champagne.

Me & My People

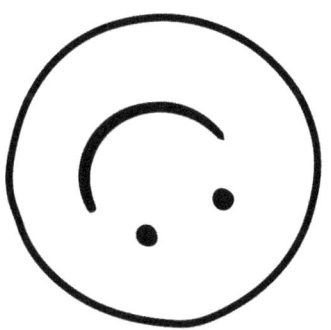

Tempest Gotta Blow

Poetry
is like
breathing.

And I've held my breath
for nearly
fifty-four,
long
years.

Beware
hurricanes
in the Atlantic.

Typhoons
in the Pacific.

When it's
ready for the show,
the tempest's
gonna blow.

The storm,
She's a comin'.

I Inherited the Gene

You know the one,
my Restless One.
The one that sent you
heavily pregnant,
toting a toddler,
my great-grandfather times thirteen,
sailing on a ship,
wild trailing arbutus.

What compelled you
to leave it all behind?
Or perhaps he made you
and then died,
like half of them did
that ill-prepared,
First Kill Winter.

I truly doubt it was all him.
Women in our family rarely do
anything they don't want to.
So husband be damned,
I'm guessing you had plenty of say
about the matter.

Either way, you went
and now
here we are.
No more Queen's propriety for us.

How'd you survive
when so many others perished?
Kept your baby boys alive
when so many of them died.

You gave Great-Granddad quite a name:
"Resolved."
Maybe I get my creative stubbornness,
something significantly better
than plain Puritan orneriness,
from you, as well.

You'd be pleased to know
I've taken your wanderlust
and headed further West,
away from the killing frost.
No more chilblains
for our children's children.

Generations hence,
you are,
and will always be,
my true Pilgrim Rock.

Cursed Gift

Up at 4:00 a.m.
in sweet sleepless,
psychic pain
as poetry, like breath,
keeps me awake.

It is a balm.
It is an ache.
A glorious gift,
a cursed curse.

I have learned the hard way
that curses become gifts
if you give them
your blessing.

Dear Emily

Miss Dickinson,
"Miss" sounds so juvenile
for a fully-grown woman,
an aged woman even,
who just happened to
choose not to be chosen.
Or perhaps, it was never
even really a choice.

Perhaps they called you
"Goody D"
like the modern-day rapper
of Colonial times.

Formalities and politesse aside,
I will simply call you "Cousin Emily,"
as the likelihood of our
kinship is quite high.
Our twinned roots rising out of
thick, deciduous lands
where Lady slippers grow
and porcupines lumber,
dragging quills in the snow.

My people lived, and still live,
just up the road apiece
from your people.
A short horse or carriage ride
away, less than a day,
even with my non-horsey math
It adds up.

As a teenager, my friends and I
would dust off our small town dirt
and drive up old Route 202
in search of thrills,
or at least the chance to
roller skate at the now-Dead Mall
or sneak into an R-rated movie.

On the way, we passed
"put money in the box,

help yourself" stands offering
early apples, sweet, sweet corn
and most precious of all,
Vine-ripened, late summer,
juice-running-down-your-chin
tomatoes.

We flew down those winding roads
like we owned them.
But they were yours
before they were ours,
or at least they were
when you were a girl still open
to exploring the world,
before words became your world.

Tell me, Cousin Emily,
when you closed that door,
did you miss our roads?
Our rough riding roads
with flocks of wild turkeys,
strutting, feathers unfurled?
Did you miss the doe and her
speckled fawn
or did they make house calls
special just for you?
What about the sour,
nose-clenching scent of skunk,
did he deliver that too?

Maybe I'm out of touch,
but I feel you missed so much.

Perhaps that was your problem:
maybe you simply
felt too much.

If that was the case,
then we must be related.

My sweet, sweet Sister Emily,
I feel for you.

Because it happens to me, too.

We24ever!

"That's the most alert newborn
I've ever seen,"
the pediatrician announced
as your big, unfocused
searching eyes
glared up at him
from the hospital bassinet.

No sleep needed for you.
Not with a new exciting world
not to be missed.
No sleep for either of us
for a long,
long,
long
time.
But, of course,
how was this new mother
to know.

I used to joke
that I should've run
for the hills
right then and there,
but instead, I was so proud.
So fucking proud
that my episiotomy stitches
practically burst.

You were only a day old
and already
exceptional.

My finest,
most divine
creation.

We24ever!
Stolen WiFi password
be damned.

I Once Was Beautiful

Such a loaded word
I feel bad even using it.
Like you will judge me
for something
that was a simple fact.

Eyes green as fresh grass
lips the new berries of June
the mirror approves

beautiful.

This wasn't something I chose.
Although I certainly wouldn't
have chosen the opposite.
That has its own real
and painful ramifications.
Even plainness is poignant.

But once upon a time,
heads snapped in the street,
a random drunk man at a fancy
restaurant handed me a rose
in front of my husband

radiant.

Mind you,
not supermodel,
tail end of the distribution
goddess,
but approachable
girl-next-door

glorious.

Scandalous in a short, short
gold lamé dress,
shapely legs,
silver heels clicking.

Grumpy old lady tsk-tsking
about where has the world gone

gorgeous.

Now I walk the path of the crone
largely unnoticed, disregarded.
Slightly wider hips swaying,
belly gently round, baby soft.
Grassy eyes brighter by far
with wisdom.

She is still here.
She is still all here
and isn't going anywhere.

There is more than one way
to set the world on fire.

Chocolate Bar

You know you want me.
I'm here.
You hid me
in your desk drawer.
Me and my nuts
are making you nuts.

Your mouth
is so inviting.
Your lips
with saliva
rising
behind them.

Those teeth,
maybe I should be afraid,
but we know
I enjoy
being bit.

We are both
deliciously
masochistic
that way.

(A girl's got to have her vices.)

Love Platelets

(dedicated to my Women's Group:
a.k.a. "Midwife Your Midlife")

You have rolled up your sleeve,
given regularly over the years.
Smiled, needle sliding into vein.
Just a little pain:
What you give, you gain.

Now your generous
chosen kin
rally, encircle you.

Gently, but firmly
they
((HOLD))
you.

And glistening,
glowing
love platelets
flow.

It's only then
you realize,
you're no longer
bleeding out.

On the Occasion
of My Daughter's College Graduation

In the third grade, you broke down sobbing:
"I will NEVER get into college!"
I tried to console your intense, anxious heart.
But you weren't having it.
You needed to catastrophize and cry.

After five hundred hours of volunteering in high school,
AP classes up the wazoo,
you got into friggin' UCLA,
full-ride scholarship.

Your freshman year was at-home Zoom classes.
Followed by sorority house highs and lows.
Ultimately you told those snooty girls where to go.

You were Roofied at a frat party.
Danced at the Grammy's After-Party on stage with Flava Flav.

Got Covid, not once, but twice, during final exams.
Had your wisdom teeth and tonsils removed.

You have survived in depths of failing physics.
Got the highest grade in Developmental Psych.

And here you are on the cusp walking across the stage,
My beautiful Bruin, all Blue & Gold.
A big Eight-Clap to you, my Girl!

It's tempting to say: "I told you so."

We've Only Just Begun

That song always makes me a little sad.

Karen Carpenter, songbird,
chanteuse extraordinaire,
devoured by her own demons.

Sometimes the most beautiful voices
disguise the deepest, darkest pain.

Note for note,
her voice resounds wistfully,
in my head.

Perhaps my voice
will stay with you, too.

We've only just begun.

Acknowledgments

This adventure started for me in October 2023 when I saw an online ad to audition for Community Literature Initiative (CLI). I was intrigued as I had dabbled in poetry and have wanted to write a book since the author Robert Cormier (*The Chocolate War*) visited my elementary school and told me I could be a writer someday.

Unfortunately, the CLI auditions were scheduled for the weekend of my women's group retreat. So I figured it wasn't meant to be. A day or two after returning from the retreat, I received an email inviting me to a makeup virtual audition. I did a little digging and CLI seemed legit, so I found a couple of poems I'd written over the years and signed up.

When CLI Founder Hiram Sim's appeared on Zoom, he asked me who my favorite poet was. It was intended to be an ice breaker question but having not read a lot of poetry, I said the first poet who popped into my mind: Robert Frost. From Hiram's seemingly lukewarm response, I guessed mine was not a popular CLI answer! Fortunately, when I read my poems, he seemed a bit more enthusiastic.

Then in true dramatic Susan Black Allen fashion, the next week had a series of whiplash highs and lows: breaking up with my boyfriend of two and half years and moving out; getting accepted into CLI; temporarily moving in with friends; attending my first CLI class; getting diagnosed with Covid and sleeping fourteen hours a day for several days.

Weirdly, while I had Covid, the words started to flow. I wasn't conscious a lot, but when I was, I found I had a lot to say, both to myself and others. I wrote about my breakup, "An Apology" and "I've Pollinated Your Garden," that week. I also wrote the eponymous poem, "The Best Sex I Never Had," then, too. So I guess Covid is good for something!

That said, I am going to attempt to thank folks who supported me and my writing in semi-chronological order.

Thank you to Hiram Sims for creating CLI and welcoming me into the fold.

Thank you to Lena Wellman and Curtis Fitzergerald for taking me in after my breakup and caring for me while I had Covid.

Thank you to Marianne Swift-Gifford for helping me move and swearing and crying with me while driving a U-Haul.

Deep appreciation and gratitude to all of the women in my Midwife Your Midlife group (aforementioned retreat participants and more). You have rooted for me loudly throughout this process and I feel the abundance of your love. A particular call-out to Debbie and John Resler, Lonna and Jon Leghart, and Mindi Marlow who moved me back into my condo – cat fur, stench and all.

Thank you also to some of my favorite people who offered support and/or read random poems texted to them day and night for the past six months including: my sister Amanda Black; Stacy Hyman; Angela Carles; Chantalle O'Donnell; Ruth Cain; Michelle Polischuk; Audrey Koke; Beth Olberding Mozell; Denise Stemmons; Mandi Lane; Donna Johnson; Dean Patterson; Mike DiLorenzo; Bart Brock; Rachel Rott; my cousin Nina Fred; Doris Bühler; and Rebecca Cutter. Smooches also to Jeff Chasin and Dorothy Derifield who are adopted family. A flock of flamingos to Mark Kistler whose warmth, generosity, and talent have recently rocked my world. If I've missed someone, please forgive me and know I love you.

A big thanks to my CLI teachers, TA, writing partners and classmates: Elle; Andrew Hartford; Anastasia Fenald; Nemesis Renta; Hope Czbas; Sierra Zounes; Shannon English; Alorah Bliese; Arwen Jamison and Paola Hornbuckle. It's been a pleasure hearing your poetry and being on this path with you. May your words find many ears.

Beyond thanks to my dear friend Jane Foley, whose fingerprints are all over this manuscript. Jane completed a full edit of this book in its rough-cut version with such love, generosity and wisdom. She is a true gem: a wonderful person and writer. I look forward to returning the editing favor someday – although I will never have your grammatical chops.

To Jane Roper, thank you for agreeing to blurb the book of an unknown newbie. I appreciate it more than you know.

Kimiko White, a.k.a. "The Hyphen Queen," your edits and enthusiasm were exactly the spit shine that my manuscript needed at the end to make it glow.

To photographer Monica Hahn and makeup artist Fatima Zapata, you worked some serious magic with my headshots. I assure you that I do not look like this at 6:00 a.m. when I'm walking my puppy in my ratty bathrobe. May they bring me online dating juju as well.

To graphic artist Kelli Urabe, thank you for transforming my crazy ideas into a book cover that brings me great joy and represents both my writing and life. I love your suggestion to use my handwriting for the title. Letting me turn the "e" in "Sex" into a clitoris is the cherry on top!

Tiffany Quon, my layout editor, thank you for your warmth, enthusiasm, professionalism and patience. I'm still deeply honored that my work reminds you of the poet, Anne Sexton. Like your favorite Emily Dickinson, I wouldn't be shocked if I am distantly related to Anne, too. We three all calling Massachusetts home.

To all who inspired these poems, I am deeply grateful to you and send you blessings. Even the deeply misguided ones and those who hurt me. Perhaps especially to them, because they likely need extra blessings and I have an abundance to share.

Lastly, thank you to my daughter Emerson "Emmy" Allen for agreeing not to read her mother's sexiest poems. We both know there just isn't therapy enough.

Previously Published Works

The following poems have previously been published.

- "Like Roses," *San Diego Annual Poetry Anthology*, 2020-2021
- "Love Remains," *San Diego Annual Poetry Anthology*, 2023-2024

About the Author

Susan Black Allen is a psychotherapist who has secretly dabbled in writing poetry for years. She has published essays and poems on mental health, relationships, and parenting in *The Boston Sunday Globe Magazine*, the *San Diego Poetry Annual Anthology*, and for the non-profit This is My Brave.

Ms. Black Allen moved to San Diego in 2015 from Boston after a winter with 110 inches of snow. She was done with all things cold and dark. With its sunshine and everblooming flowers, San Diego is now one of the top loves of her life. She's pretty fond of her daughter Emmy, cat Finn, and puppy Poppy, too.

www.ingramcontent.com/pod-product-compliance
Lightning Source LLC
Chambersburg PA
CBHW051318120626
46547CB00015B/2289